Baboons on the Runway

2007-8 NMI
MISSION EDUCATION RESOURCES

✳ ✳ ✳

BOOKS

AFRICA'S SOUL HOPE
The AIDS Crisis and the Church
by Ellen Decker

BABOONS ON THE RUNWAY
And Other Humorous Stories from Africa
by Richard F. Zanner

MEETING JESUS
by Keith Schwanz

THE NUDGE IN MY SIDE
Stories from Indonesia and the Philippines
by The Bob McCroskeys

THEY SAW ONLY FEET
More Life Lessons from Missionary Kids
by Dean Nelson

A LOVE STORY FROM TRINIDAD
by Ruth O. Saxon

✳ ✳ ✳

ADULT MISSION EDUCATION RESOURCE BOOK

RESPONDING TO MISSION CHALLENGES
Editors: Aimee Curtis and Rosanne Bolerjack

Baboons on the Runway
and other Humorous Stories from Africa

by
Richard F. Zanner

Nazarene Publishing House
Kansas City, Missouri

Copyright 2007
Nazarene Publishing House

ISBN-13: 978-0-8341-2293-2
ISBN-10: 0-8341-2293-6

Printed in the United States of America

Editor: Aimee Curtis
Cover Design: J.R. Caines
Interior Design: Sharon Page

10 9 8 7 6 5 4 3 2 1

Dedication

This book is dedicated to my four children and nine grandchildren who enjoy hearing the stories of my exploits in Africa.

Acknowledgment

A special word of thanks to Mrs. Kitty Voges
for typing the manuscript.

Contents

Dr. Richard F. Zanner, regional director emeritus for the Church of the Nazarene in Africa, is presently heading a foundation called Edu-Care International.

A native of Bavaria, Germany, Richard went to Johannesburg, South Africa, in 1953 on a full scholarship to study mining engineering. After graduation, he enrolled in and graduated from Nazarene Theological College. He married Valerie in 1954. Richard and Valerie were called back to Germany during 1960 to assist in pioneering the work of the denomination in Europe.

While pastoring, Richard took further studies at Frankfurt University and became cofounder of the European Nazarene Bible College in Switzerland, now European Nazarene College.

After 9 years in the pastorate, Richard was elected district superintendent of the Middle-European district in 1969. He served in that capacity for 11 years. During that time, he was also elected president of the Evangelical Alliance in Frankfurt (8 years) and denominational youth leader for Europe (8 years).

In 1978, MidAmerica Nazarene University conferred the doctor of divinity degree on him in Zurich, Switzerland.

In 1980, Dr. Zanner was appointed regional director of Africa for the Church of the Nazarene. Under his leadership the church expanded and entered 25 additional countries on the continent. Africa Nazarene University in Nairobi, Kenya, honored him with a doctor of letters degree in 1999.

Author of numerous articles and books, including *No Other Gospel* and *Night Hunt in Kisumi,* Dr. Richard F. Zanner also served as executive editor for the German magazine, *Perspektiven* (11 years), and for the *Trans-African,* the official church magazine for the continent of Africa (18 years).

Richard and Valerie reside in Johannesburg. They have three daughters and a son. All children are married, and the Zanners enjoy nine grandchildren.

Foreword

For nearly 20 years I sat in strategic planning meetings with Richard; these were meetings where discussion was intense on finding the most appropriate ways to start, develop, and multiply the church. It was all about the fulfillment of the Great Commission through the Church of the Nazarene throughout the entire world. I found Richard to be consumed with that passion. But it wasn't present in just meetings; this passion was also part of his thoughts and purpose in everything he did. I also sat next to him at many meals, on trains, boats, and airplanes, and once again that passion was always there, and he was always on the move. Those times together took place in legendary cities and "far away places" throughout the world.

Once I spent two weeks driving in a car with him. His dynamic personality and whirlwind style of work was amazing to watch. I found myself caught up in his positive, fast-paced drive to do his best and give his all for the mission of the church. His purpose for life and work was then, and still is today, very clear: he serves the Lord and the Church of the Nazarene in every aspect of his life. Richard's legacy as pastor and district superintendent in his native Germany, and his 20 years as regional director for the Africa Region, continue to be exemplary and will bear fruit for generations to come. Already we see it happening on the continent of Africa.

How appropriate he chose to write about missionaries from the great African Nazarene family—the people he loves, labored for in the Kingdom, rejoiced with in their triumphs, and wept with in their sorrows.

Missionaries are soldiers in the army of the Lord, but rarely does one think of the smiling soldier. If you know the author, then you know this "soldier of the Lord" has a twinkle in his eye. His stories are riveting, often fun to read. He shares his thoughts from one who is so caught up in his ministry that on one hand he is the "soldier fighting for good" and on the other hand "the simply delightful Christian." Here are stories of an international Nazarene who is obviously enjoying being in the action of Christian ministry. I find this book full of joy, often fun, other times thought provoking, but always captivating.

John M. Smee
Caribbean Regional Director

Introduction

The world of missions is a colorful, exciting, and multifaceted world. Nobody who has ever been involved with missions would deny that. Indeed, it is probably the most exhilarating sector of the Church of Jesus Christ.

Within the world of missions, there exists a band of God's servants who, in the pursuit of God's call, live in other cultures and find themselves somewhere on this globe, singing the song of victory, throwing out the net, calling people to the Cross. Sometimes alone, often in the company of others, but always with God on their side, they stand on the front line, in the first trench of spiritual warfare. We call them missionaries.

These men and women, both young and old, leave behind the comforts, securities, and conveniences of their own cultures and once more experience a growing-up process, this time as adults.

Like a baby, they learn a new language. They become acquainted with new circumstances, acquire knowledge of new traditions, begin to appreciate other cultures, and develop new friendships— all in the service of the Lord Jesus Christ. Their equipment? The blessing of God and the support of the church.

Dr. Zanner *(standing in the center)*
with pastors in Mozambique.

When I arrived in Africa in 1980, I had no idea
what would be waiting for me. I had previously
prayed for missionaries, given to missions,
preached on missions, and done my best as a minis-
ter to motivate Christians toward mission-minded-
ness.

When I set foot on African soil, my mandate
was to establish the first regional office for the
Church of the Nazarene in the world and to guide
Nazarene mission efforts throughout the continent
of Africa.

Most of the missionaries in Africa were North
Americans with a sprinkling of personnel from the

United Kingdom. I was a continental European, a German national, whose culture and traditions were as alien to them as theirs was to me. My English was fluent, but it was my second language, and it had neither the broad nonchalant North American flavor nor the melodious and sophisticated-sounding inflection with its rising intonations as the British. The Africa missionary family welcomed me pleasantly, yet inwardly they felt as nervous about my leadership as I was about my new role.

Then I made a liberating discovery: the world of missions, while many times serious and solemn, is also full of humor and laughter. I must admit this was stress-relieving, healing therapy that provided emotional balance and reduced the strain in some rather challenging situations. Proverbs 17:22, "A cheerful heart is good medicine, but a crushed spirit dries up the bones," became a constant companion, a much-appreciated reassurance from God's Word in my life.

There were many occasions during my tenure in Africa where humor helped me and laughter lifted me above predicaments. It helped me not to take myself too importantly and guided me to find new and profoundly healthy perspectives.

The following pages will introduce you to many of these hilarious situations and experiences. I share events that, for the lack of a better description, can only be called "safety valves for people under steam." Some of these episodes have spiritual conclusions while others, though lacking in spiritual application, provided an opportunity for judgment and decision.

Woven through it all, however, is the golden thread of God's unending love, His passion to save souls, and His forgiving nod for the shortcomings of His servants. My intention is to give glory to God for what has been accomplished and to reflect on missionaries as the true soldiers of Christ. But I also want to portray that even on the mission field "we cook only with water" as we aspire to become the best for God. This is an anthem to fun, family, and fellowship.

I ask forgiveness if anyone feels uncomfortable by anything I share. I have learned to laugh at myself and this, at times, has provided healing. If you discover a clown in any of the tales, the clown am I. God, I am sure, had many occasions to smile or snicker or even laugh out loud when He looked upon the stumblings of this, His eager servant.

Richard F. Zanner

Baboons on the Runway

"This is Lear Jet on finals," a voice crackled in my cockpit radio. "I think you have baboons on the runway. I will have to abort and go around."

How did I get into this dilemma? Let me explain.

Missionary Marilyn Willis,* editor of the *Trans-African* magazine, wanted to run a story on the beginning of aviation in Africa. At the time I was the only pilot in the region. Marilyn, better known as Lyn, requested a couple of pictures for the article. Missionary David Moyer, a good photographer, suggested that he take his equipment and accompany me to the airport where we would request permission for him to take photos of a few of my takeoffs and landings.

After arriving at the airport, I did my preflight inspection and entered the Cessna 206 with David.

---

*Marilyn Willis married Dr. Kenneth Grider in 2004 and now lives in the United States.

We asked for taxi clearance and then requested permission for David to alight from the plane at the end of the runway to set up position for taking photos while I would fly a couple of circuits. It would take a few go-arounds since David wanted to find the right position to take quality shots.

Laughter boomed in the radio from the tower. "Negative, those are not baboons. It's a dumb photographer."

Having received clearance with caution to be careful of other aircraft, we taxied out to the runway where David got off. I then began my first take-off run, rotated, and started to climb for the circuit pattern of the airport. Coming around, joining right base, and then banking, I saw David with his camera running up and down the landing strip, obviously seeking the best position. I did my touch-and-go and was up for the second circuit when I heard a clatter on the radio. It was another pilot coming through, the captain of a Lear Jet, calling the tower. The controller told the Lear Jet pilot that there was a Cessna in the circuit, but since the Lear Jet was so much faster he was given permission to be first for landing. I took the power back to slow my plane down when I heard the Lear Jet captain speaking on the radio again with a rather exasperated voice, talking about baboons on the runway.

Laughter boomed in the radio from the tower. "Negative, those are not baboons. It's a dumb photographer taking photos of another aircraft."

Silence from the cockpit of the Lear Jet, then a mumble, "Baboons . . . photographers . . . same thing!"

When I turned to descend a little later I was still laughing so hard that I almost had to abort my landing. David, bent down with his camera equipment, was charging up and down the runway while the Lear Jet taxied to a stop.

Needless to say, this brave missionary endured much teasing from his colleagues as I saw to it that the story made its rounds for many years to come.

Navigator in Nigeria

A general superintendent as a jet navigator? Read on!

Part of my responsibilities in Africa included preparing for visits from general superintendents. My goal was to make these trips comfortable, convenient, and safe, but I always looked for at least one opportunity to travel into areas where formerly no other general superintendent had gone.

At this particular time, the church in Africa was growing at such a rapid pace that we found it difficult to introduce our general church leaders to all of the newly occupied spiritual and geographical territories. Yet we felt it important that our people, especially those who were young in the faith and new in the denomination, should meet the leadership of the church, thus giving them the bigger picture of the global organization.

In planning for these visits, my office arranged the schedules and flights for each of the leaders. A designated field director (now field strategy coordinator) would meet the general superintendent and be his guide.

This time it was General Superintendent Dr. Jerald Johnson who came, and the country was Nigeria. We had an established district in the southeast corner of the country, about three hours by car north of Port Harcourt.

John Seaman, then field director, and I met Dr. Johnson in Lagos, the largest city of the country. Transferring from the international airport to the domestic airport, though only three miles away, is an event in itself. But we made it and soon found ourselves in the domestic lounge, five hours before our plane was scheduled to take off for Port Harcourt. We would be met by our Nazarene leaders there and then travel the approximately three hours by car to Abak.

To be early was vital. Printed schedules can mean very little. If enough passengers to fill a plane were present, it would take off. Conversely, if not enough passengers were ready, the flight would be delayed.

We eventually boarded the aircraft and scrambled for available seats as possessing a boarding pass meant absolutely nothing. We breathed a sigh of relief and committed ourselves to God for a safe journey and to the pilot for a good takeoff and an uneventful landing at our destination.

The three of us used the time for a kind of orientation chat about the forthcoming program. Dr. Johnson sat by the window, I was next to him, and across the aisle was John. The weather, normal for this part of West Africa, was hot and humid with temperatures about 100 degrees Fahrenheit. Low clouds and that peculiar West African haze engulfed us soon after takeoff. Throughout the flight we could not see anything, not even the tip of the aircraft's wing.

On descent to Port Harcourt we strapped ourselves in again and fell silent, each alone with his thoughts and emotions. John and I, having had years of travel in West Africa, silently prayed for a safe landing while Dr. Johnson looked out of the window, waiting for the clouds to break.

The usual crackle in the loudspeaker system prepared us for an announcement. A rather sonorous and pleasant voice speaking in heavily accented English said, "This is your captain speaking. We trust you have enjoyed the flight so far. We are on descent to Port Harcourt. Unfortunately, two weeks ago, an airliner crashed on landing and took out all of the ILS (Instrument Landing System) that is still under repair. We are close to the airport now, and I will begin circling. I request all of you who are sitting at the windows to look out and help us find the airport. We hope to break cloud in a few moments. If you see the airport, please contact the flight attendant immediately. Thank you."

Dr. Johnson turned to me and said, "I like it here. This pilot has humor."

"What do you mean?" I retorted. "The captain is serious, Dr. Johnson."

"Ha-ha! I may be new to Nigeria, but I am not new to this world . . ."

"This, Dr. Johnson, is our world, and our world is another world. We better look out of the window and try to find the airport."

Dr. Johnson looked at John Seaman who nodded his head. Then turning back to me Dr. Johnson said, "You cannot be serious."

"I may not be, but the pilot is."

We did break through the clouds after a few more anxious moments. Between the top of 60-foot-high palm trees and the cloud base, we had a clearance of perhaps 300 to 400 feet. The pilot held the aircraft very evenly as the circles became wider and wider. Passengers on both sides strained their necks, each trying to be the first one to shout, "I've found it!"

After about 10 minutes, we heard the crackle in the loudspeaker again, "Ladies and gentlemen, this is the captain. We have not sighted Port Harcourt yet, and we are beginning to run low on fuel. We will make one more circle, and if we do not find the airport this time, we will have to divert to Calabar, about 35 minutes away. We apologize for any inconvenience that this may cause you. Please continue to look for the airport."

"WAWA," John said as he turned to the general superintendent.

"What does that mean?" Dr. Johnson asked anxiously.

"'West Africa Wins Again.' Welcome to our world."

My thought-wheels began spinning. The district superintendent and secretary were coming to Port Harcourt to meet us for the drive to the church in Abak. Nobody would be in Calabar. How would we make it from there or notify anyone with no telephones available? And who would preach to the 800 to 1,000 people gathered for this special occasion? If we landed in Calabar, would we have to entrust our leader to one of those taxis that, due to the luggage on the roof, are usually higher than they are long?

The crackling in the loudspeaker interrupted my thinking.

"Hallelujah! The copilot spotted the airport. We

will be landing in a few minutes. Please make sure that your seat belts are fastened."

"What a relief. We made it," said Dr. Johnson.

"Not quite," John Seaman said with a broad smile. "We only say that when we are safely on the ground."

"At least our pilot is a Christian. That makes a difference," Dr. Johnson smiled.

"Let's ask him after landing," I retorted.

Indeed, the landing was good, but as we taxied to our holding place on the runway we noticed the crashed Nigerian airliner. That aircraft had broken into three parts, but apparently it had not caught fire. We also saw the damage to the runway lights and the ILS system.

As we disembarked onto a wet tarmac with drizzle in the air, Dr. Johnson stretched and announced, "Well, so much for a general superintendent as navigator."

With a smirk on his face, John Seaman replied, "Yes, he may have been the navigator, but he never found the airport."

Just then the captain came out, and I ventured to ask him if indeed he was a Christian. He looked at me rather quizzically and replied, "Not really. But the situation in the cockpit would have almost caused me to become one."

What a welcome sight it was to see our Nazarene friends standing there, welcoming us to this part of the world.

While preaching, Dr. Johnson related our experience, trying to elicit laughter from the people. How surprised he was to find them just nodding as if to say, "Nothing unusual, nothing special, just part of life."

The Departure of Elijah

Our visit to the church in Abak, Nigeria, had more than one purpose. While we wanted to emphasize the great global thrust of our denomination by introducing our general superintendent, we also wanted to participate in their first assembly and election of a district superintendent. An installation service was to follow.

The incumbent district superintendent was a great old man by the name of Ekaidem. I had met him for the first time almost 10 years earlier when he was pastor of a large church. He was ancient then, I thought, but now, almost a decade later, having been appointed as district superintendent during the embryonic stage of the Nigeria Southeast District, it was time for him to step down.

Rev. Ekaidem was not only old, he was also a sickly man who could not see well and whose walk was more a shuffle supported by a heavy stick. We did not know his age—I do not think even he knew his age. We also did not want to hurt him, embarrass him, or make things difficult for him. He had a large family and, surprisingly, still a few younger children at home.

We loved the old gentleman and appreciated the work he had done for God and the church throughout his lifetime. But now it was time for a successor to take his place.

John Seaman and I sat down with Brother Ekaidem. Three of the senior pastors on the district also joined us. We talked to him, guided him, and tried to help him see there was no alternative.

We also helped him to understand that upon election of a new district superintendent, we would have not only an installation service but also a recognition service for him and his many years of ministry. This would be a climax for his ministry. Eventually, Brother Ekaidem agreed.

We enjoyed a great district assembly, the first for our constituency in that region. When the people learned they would have a say in choosing a leader, they were overjoyed. In fact, they became so carried away with the privilege of electing other church officials that they lifted the candidates in the air on chairs, cheering them on and proclaiming their good qualities. It became quite a show.

Both the general superintendent and I had taken our jackets off. It was hot. It was muggy. It was loud. Our voices became hoarse. Brother John on the other side did his bit so that order, to at least some degree, prevailed.

Then came the election of the new district superintendent. There were two candidates. One was Rev. O. A. Udoh, a former customs officer at Lagos Airport who had been most generous to the church and was greatly revered by the people. The other was a highly esteemed and respected senior pastor.

After two sincere attempts to have a normal election by ballot—only to find that individuals voted with three or four ballots—we discarded that modus operandi and came up with a new system. One candidate received a blue tag and the other candidate a red tag. John had a cardboard box with the color red, and I had a cardboard box with the color blue.

We posted ourselves in a room with two doors and allowed all eligible delegates to pass through the room where only John and I stood with the two boxes. All delegates received specially prepared pieces of paper—they did not have to write or mark anything. They simply came in one door, put their ballot into either John's box or mine, and walked out the other door.

Outside of the voting room in the big auditorium, the general superintendent stood and made sure the delegates exiting the voting room took their seats again and didn't return to the line for a second vote.

This way we elected brother O. A. Udoh and were ever so glad when it was all over. We felt triumphant, happy, and victorious—though physically exhausted by the time we finished at about four o'clock in the afternoon.

Now came the final, crowning experience: the installation service, which was also to be a farewell service expressing gratitude to Rev. Ekaidem.

Dr. Johnson, being an innovative leader, had a brilliant idea. We would have two chairs decorated with flowers on the platform in the evening service. One would be for the outgoing district superintendent, Rev. Ekaidem, and the other would be for the incoming district superintendent, Rev. Udoh. John and I would sit behind them on the platform, one to the right and one to the left, ready to assist at any time should it become necessary. Dr. Johnson planned to preach on Elijah and Elisha with the title of the sermon being, "Let Thy Mantel Fall on Him."

To make this as dramatic as possible, and to illustrate vividly what was happening, we borrowed a colorful and beautiful blanket from one of the ladies. That blanket would be on the shoulders of Elijah, the outgoing superintendent. At a given moment during the service, Dr. Johnson would lift the mantel from the shoulders of Rev. Ekaidem and put it on the shoulders of Elisha, the incoming district superintendent. All of us were excited about the service. We knew it would be unique, blessed, and rewarding.

The church building was not yet complete. Windows had no panes, and the doors only had temporary fixtures. Crudely carpeted pews filled about half of the auditorium with people standing and sitting on the floor beyond.

We had forgotten that the church out there in the jungle had no electric lights. The parsonage next door had a generator that was able to provide enough power for four or five bulbs. We worked quickly to put a cable from the house to these few bulbs strung across the front of the church and

An African congregation meeting outdoors

added a few candles. Nevertheless, the church, being filled with more than 800 people, only had light for the first 20 feet or so. Dr. Johnson decided not to preach from the pulpit, but to stand right under the lightbulbs so he could read the Bible with the two district superintendents behind him and the congregation in the darkness before him.

After much singing and praying the general superintendent began to preach. It was a beautifully structured message to which there was audible response from the invisible crowd.

Dr. Johnson's preaching was building to the climax, riding high on the responses from the congregation. And it seemed that he almost forgot about the four of us sitting behind him.

The service, in true African fashion, had gone on for a long time, and Rev. Ekaidem, with the colorful blanket around his shoulders simply had to obey nature's call. He got up and, stick in one hand, blanket in the other, slowly shuffled to the back door and into the darkness.

With a dramatic sweep, the preacher turned around and moved toward—an empty chair.

There was nothing unusual about it, except that the preacher was totally unaware of what was happening behind him. John and I exchanged rather frantic glances, hoping that Dr. Johnson would continue for a while and give Rev. Ekaidem a chance to get back. Wishful thinking indeed!

Dr. Johnson moved from the left to the right, his open Bible in one hand, exhorting God's Word. Soon he came to the climax by saying, ". . . and this is what we are doing here tonight, asking God to bless Elisha as he has blessed Elijah. And so we plead for a double portion of God's grace as we take the mantle from the shoulders of Elijah, putting it onto the shoulders of Elisha."

With a dramatic sweep that would have graced the finest matador in a Spanish bullfighting arena, the preacher turned around and moved toward—an empty chair. Elijah had not come back yet.

I will never forget the expression on Dr. Johnson's face. Aghast, he was silent for a moment and then hoarsely whispered to us, "Where is Elijah?"

Thankful for the dim light and the encroaching darkness where we were sitting so that our faces could not be seen clearly, neither John nor I could speak for a moment, for we shook with laughter.

There he was, a great leader of our great denomination with a great message. The stage all set for the dramatic switch, changing one era in the history of the Nigerian church for another. But the main actor was missing.

Eventually I collected myself enough to quietly whisper back, "Elijah has gone to the toilet."

Dr. Johnson, quick-witted, turned around to the congregation with a new approach, "As Elijah had been taken to heaven, so Rev. Ekaidem has moved gracefully away to make room for Brother Udoh, our new district superintendent. Once more we say thank you, Brother Ekaidem, thank you, Elijah, for vacating the chair as we say welcome, Rev. Udoh, welcome, Elisha. May a double portion rest upon your shoulders."

And with that great theatrical gesture again, Dr. Johnson made his sweeping bow, left hand holding the Bible, and turned around to find Elijah back in his chair. Rev. Ekaidem had shuffled in and taken his seat again.

First a hush, then like a breeze of wind rustling up the leaves of trees, a crescendo of laughter that could no longer be suppressed swept like a giant wave through the darkness. I chuckle as I remember the scene. We closed the service with prayer. An exhausted, breathless general superintendent took it bravely on the cheek.

Let me add that Rev. Ekaidem was a gracious old man until the Lord took him home to heaven about two years later. Rev. Udoh became one of the finest district superintendents in the Church of the Nazarene. It was my honor and privilege, together with John Seaman, to officiate at his farewell service about 10 years later.

Will anyone hold it against us—surely the Lord does not—that general superintendent Dr. J. D. Johnson had to "endure" us for the rest of his days in Africa? Every time the subject came up, we would burst into laughter—all at the expense of our leader. In fairness to him, he never held it against us. Dr. Johnson led the way in showing us that he could laugh at himself. On the other hand, I'm not sure that he ever shared this experience with his colleagues. If he did, they never indicated it.

Lord, Multiply This Goat!

The mist of the night phantoms faded into the rising African sun. The multitude of frogs croaking at the lakeside had long been silenced. But the "twee-twee-twee" of crickets, sometimes more melodious, sometimes just plain noisy, provided backdrop orchestration until the curtain of the dark finally lifted.

I got out of bed, discarded the sheet with which I had been covered—anything heavier would have been unbearable during the hot night—stretched my limbs and popped over to the window. Gazing out toward the great lake, I watched as the last fog banks dissolved into the first rays of the sun like sugar in coffee. What a beautiful picture I was privileged to behold again. Yes, this would be another wonderful day in central Africa—and Palm Sunday at that, one week before Easter.

Just then I heard a grunt and, looking in the direction of the sound, I saw a three-ton hippo munching away in the back garden. The fence had been trampled down. The creature normally would have been back in the water by daybreak. However, it had apparently become over-enthralled by the lettuce and the cabbages in the backyard of this house on the shore of Lake Malawi. With another grunt, my early morning visitor stomped out of the garden.

On that Sunday morning I would preach for the first time in a small, struggling Nazarene church not too far away. My topic: the entry of Jesus into Jerusalem, a picture I wanted to use to illustrate that things do change when Jesus comes.

As I later stood in the pulpit of that little church with about 50 people in the congregation, I asked rhetorical questions: "Do you believe change comes when Jesus enters your life? Are you able to trust Him in your own life for miracles to happen? Have you experienced His power since He washed your sins away? Will you believe with me and allow Him to give you a vision for your own life, for your family, and for your church?"

As I preached, an almost revolutionary thought took hold of me. This little church had a pastor who lived with his family far below the subsistence level. The congregation had never been able to make ends meet. In these rural areas, people had little money—almost none. And one week from today on Easter Sunday the mission offering would be taken.

I had done my homework. I knew about the minute income of this church. How could we still challenge the people to give?

And then, without giving it much thought, I blurted out, "Our God is a God of miracles. He put this world in place. He created man and beast. He painted the beautiful landscape in which we find ourselves on this magnificent Palm Sunday morning.

"Yes, He expects us to believe in miracles. But at the same time, He also has demands. He wants us to do our part. Believing, kneeling, and praying is not all there is to faith. He has given us hands to work, legs and feet to walk, heads to think, and hearts to believe.

"I want to challenge all of you here this morning. Next Sunday is Easter Sunday—our resurrection celebration. Jesus has risen. In our denomination we have declared Easter Sunday as a special day on which we think of others. In every Nazarene church around the world, we will take up an offering that will help send missionaries to reach people with God's love.

"If you will trust me this morning, if you pledge to work with me and do as I instruct, I promise you a miracle next Sunday. I fly back to Johannesburg tomorrow. It is a two-hour flight, a very long way, but I promise to be back next Sunday to rejoice with you over what God will do with us and through us.

Do you have the faith and the courage to follow me?"

I saw the sparkle in their eyes. I noticed the smile on their faces. I observed the wonderment, the questioning in their expressions, but I also knew they would commit themselves to step out in faith to follow their leader.

I sensed I was on the winning course. I took a new "tack" in my message. I set the sails into the wind.

"Jesus gave His life on Good Friday," I continued. "He went to the Cross and sacrificed His all for you and me. I want all of us, including myself, to bring a sacrifice for Him next Sunday. Now I understand that you may not have much money to give. I know there are only few men in this congregation who have jobs. But all of us have something: gardens, vegetables, chickens, and perhaps even a goat. Jesus does not ask what we have. Instead He tells us to give of what we have.

"So here is the plan: You bring every potato that you can spare, as well as maize stalks, carrots, cabbages, anything that grows in your garden for the kitchen pot. You can even bring chickens, small ones, big ones, old ones, young ones. You can bring eggs—anything that can be eaten. Then invite your neighbors. Tell them I will be coming back from Johannesburg. Tell them that it is going to be an unusual service. Tell them that this church is going to experience something that is bigger than ourselves."

When I left the next morning, almost the whole congregation bid me good-bye and promised to do as we had decided. I left fulfilled and rewarded. All the way to Johannesburg I prayed that God would bless our efforts.

Easter was soon upon us. I arrived on Saturday and again had a good night's rest at the lakeshore house. The pastor assured me the people had been in and out and back and forth, bringing their potatoes and their carrots. They had done their part in the project. Now it was up to me.

I quickly corrected the pastor and said that it was not up to me—I would just show the way. God himself would add His blessings.

When I entered the church that Easter Sunday morning, I was completely overwhelmed by what I saw. The whole platform was filled with plastic bags full of vegetables, sugar sacks full of potatoes, and mounds of carrots, tomatoes, and onions. I even spied a cardboard box which, upon closer examination, smelled suspiciously. I opened it and discovered it was three quarters full of fish—the famous Jambo of Lake Malawi. It is a delicious fish, and every visitor to Malawi asks for it. But was this the place to store fish? We had no refrigeration, no cool room, and it was a rather hot Sunday morning. This did not quite fit into my plan. I had not known that among the congregation there was also a fisherman. He brought what he had, just as he was asked to do.

But that was not all. In front of the pulpit a dozen chickens flapped their wings, making quite a noise. Their legs had been tied, but their mouths were open. Just behind them, a male goat with two short, but formidable, horns was tied to the pulpit. Its lamentations and the cackle from the chickens made quite a racket.

Yes, I had to strain. Not only was the platform and the space before the pulpit full of produce and livestock, but the people had also brought their neighbors and the neighbors' kids. The church was filled to the brim, expectant eyes on this poor servant of the Lord whose attempts to preach found echo again and again from the chatter of the children, the amens and hallelujahs of the grown-ups, the cackling of the hens, and the bleating of our goat. All of that together with my message, a cacophony of sounds, would have graced any village market on a busy day.

Somehow I made it through my sermon and concluded with the second part of my challenge. Since the next day would be Easter Monday, a holiday, we would meet for special prayer. Tuesday morning I would meet the congregation at six o'clock to load up evenly divided consignments and station ourselves on the main roads leading out of town. I put the ladies in charge of selling our goods while the men and children waved down passing motorists, making them aware of the bargains we offered.

Each party also received a few chickens among all the garden produce, and I retained the goat for the part that I was to lead. Yes, I, too, would stand out there with my troop and do my best.

Tuesday morning came and found us positioned. Everybody had great fun as the kids and men waved down all the cars that came along, and the ladies sold, bargained, and bartered at the top of their voices. It was not difficult to stop people driving by. They saw this little mountain of garden produce, the ladies in their colorful outfits, and the kids with their "Malawi kebabs" (field mice impaled on a sharpened branch—a delicious meal for the local population).

Indeed, the produce went fast and so did the chickens, but we still had the goat. Eventually, a Mercedes Benz with two Asian businessmen stopped. I pleaded with them to buy the goat and did my best to recount the benefits of the animal, painting a picture of the delicious meat it would make since it was a rather young specimen. Eventually they agreed and paid the money we asked for it. We tied the feet of the goat, heaved it into the trunk of the car, said a polite thank-you, and waved them good-bye.

I saw the brake lights of the Mercedes Benz in the distance. The car was turning around.

In the pose of a victor, I clapped my hands, smiled at my courageous crew, and readied myself to pack up and leave for the church where we had arranged to meet after our big sale. Just then I saw the brake lights of the Mercedes Benz in the distance. The car was turning around.

I had a terrible foreboding. The car came back and stopped in front of us. The gentleman on the driver's side got out and said, "Sir, this is impossible. Listen to that noise from the trunk. We are sorry. We are on our way to Lilongwe, and it is a long ride. This animal of yours is making such a racket that we can neither listen to the radio nor talk to each other. We want to give it back to you."

"Please don't do that," I pleaded. "It would be so disappointing to these dear people. We have already rejoiced and thanked God for the money you gave us. Do not do this to us now. A deal is a deal."

In my eager attempts to prevent a return of sale, I did not hear what they were trying to say.

Eventually it registered: "You can keep the money, but also keep the goat."

Now we really rejoiced. After expressing profusely our gratitude and waving friendly good-byes once more, we went home and met the others at the church. We thanked God, for they, too, had sold their produce. The Lord not only blessed our efforts, honored our faith, and gave us great joy, He also provided us with a fine roast for the festive occasion.

We feasted, sang, prayed, and laughed into the night. When we counted the money, all were greatly astonished, even shocked. We had more than double the amount of the total income of this little church for the entire previous year.

When I left to fly home the next day, I exhorted the pastor to preach a sermon on the faithfulness of God the following Sunday.

"Tell your people, as well as those whom they brought along, that God honored what we did in a special way. Tell them that if they are faithful to God, He will be faithful to them." I gave him Hebrews 13:16 as the text for his message: "And do not forget to do good and to share with others, for with such sacrifices God is pleased."

A few years later, I saw the pastor again at a Bible college event. He had since moved to another church but greeted me with these words, "Doctor, God is good. My faith is strong. Sometimes when the devil tells me all is in vain, I hear the cackling of the hens and the bleating of the goat, and I see you standing with us by the roadside selling potatoes, chickens, and a goat. I then am always reassured in my heart that He who gave us a goat, helped us sell it, allowed us to have the money, and then gave the goat back to us will never leave nor forsake me."

Has This 5 Missionary Gone Crazy?

Conspiracy! Can you believe it happens even among missionaries?

At the beginning of my assignment as regional director for Africa, I was entrenched in the process of establishing an office, looking for facilities, gathering staff—and being very serious about it all.

One of my first official decisions was to transfer a fine missionary, David B. Moyer (now retired), to our fledgling regional office. He turned out to become one of the chief pranksters in Africa making sure that I, the newcomer, loosened up.

David set up a plan with Jack Riley, one of the senior missionaries. Jack had ministered among the Zulu people all of his adult life. The time had come, however, when we did not need missionaries in that area any longer, and thus we transferred him further south to Ciskei (now a part of South Africa) to establish a new work among the Khosa people, a subethnic group of the Zulus. The language was related, and that was an advantage for Jack. However, he and his wife, Mary Lou, had such a passion and love toward the Zulu people that they found themselves in an emotional upheaval over the transfer.

As a result, David and Jack conspired and planned the following scenario. One morning in early 1981 David came into the "holiest of holy" (his description of my office), letter in hand, face ash-gray, and said, "Sorry to disturb you, but this is really serious."

He handed me a letter from Jack, on official letterhead and all. As I read it, my face became ash-gray.

He handed me a letter from Jack, on official letterhead and all. As I read it, my face also became ash-gray. Jack was telling me he now knew beyond a shadow of a doubt that God was not happy with my decision to transfer him to Ciskei. Since God's will was more important than the regional director's desire, he and Mary Lou would leave that same evening never to return.

What followed was his rationale, which consisted of a couple of "confirmations" he had received:

Confirmation one: Jack had a dream the previous night in which I appeared as a little mouse before the throne of God. Jack and Mary Lou were kneeling before the throne with arms stretched out.

God addressed the mouse with a serious reprimand, rebuking him for disregarding the instincts of a senior missionary. The dream ended with God saying to Jack, "I want you to leave this place before the sun goes down."

Confirmation two: Jack wanted to make sure the dream was from God, so he took his Bible, put his finger between the pages, and opened it to the passage his finger had chosen. There he read Isaiah 52:11, "Depart, depart, go out from there!" He stated further that he was accustomed to ask God for such direct pronouncements throughout his ministry as a missionary. He used this method in his personal devotions and also when he prepared his sermons.

David was still standing there while I called for the secretary to get on the phone and book the next flight to Ciskei for me. I had to see this missionary immediately. On my way out of the office I yelled for David to call my wife and tell her I would not be home that night. While I threw a couple of things into my briefcase, I also asked him to get my car. He would have to go with me and drive the car back from the airport since there would not be time for me to park it before catching my flight.

Halfway down the stairs, David quickly confessed that he and Jack had set me up to break me in. I was almost completely downstairs before all of this sunk in. I sat down on the staircase, still panting, and fixed my stare on David who wisely remained a few steps out of my reach. After a while, the humorous side of it dawned on me, and laughing at myself brought relief to my racing pulse.

This incident was my introduction to missionary humor. The spiritual application I extracted from it was to relax in what you are doing—even on the mission field. Do not only pray together, but also learn to laugh together.

Surrounded by Submachine Guns!

Flying in Africa has its own special hassles. One has to get used to the weather and beacons that sometimes become dysfunctional. Voices of air-traffic controllers with accents strongly flavored by African, French, or Portuguese intonations can be confusing. Landing strips that are dented inwardly or outwardly, depending if warthogs dug a hole or ants built a hill, can be dangerous. The following is a story of one of our Nazarenes in Volunteer Service (now Mission Corps) pilots, Anton Hol. Anton came to Africa after flying for a touring outfit in the Bahamas. What a change! Anton is a great guy. Not only personality-wise, but also skill-wise. He can take an airplane apart and put it back together again; he can take it up, and he can bring it down safely.

On this particular day, Anton was en route from Johannesburg to the north of Mozambique. Richard, my son, was building a church there, and

Anton's plane was loaded with appliances and two passengers, both of whom had never been in a small aircraft. One was Richard's architect from Italy, a man well-acquainted with Africa since he had previously lived in Ethiopia. The other was an African mason, a great builder from Richard's company who had been in different countries around the continent but never in a small aircraft.

Anton was flying north when, about two hours out of Johannesburg, he noticed a smell like burning plastic in the cockpit. When he saw thin plumes of smoke coming from the dashboard, he realized that something was radically wrong with the electricals and switched them off immediately. He would have to put the plane down as long as there was still battery power left since power supply to all instruments was now shut down.

The weather was overcast, and Anton gently put the plane into a shallow descent, all the while straining his eyes for cloud break to make a landing. Inwardly praying, outwardly calm so as to not alarm his passengers, Anton went through all of the required procedures.

Suddenly, as the Cessna 206 came through the cloud base, he saw it: a beautiful landing strip right ahead, apparently belonging to a mine. A miracle in the northern province. Anton's heart was beating faster. He breathed a prayer of thanks, knowing that with a mine close by they would not have to walk through the bush or the wilderness to find help.

What Anton did not know was that the strip belonged to a diamond mine, and on that morning it was on high alert. From time-to-time these huge walk-in vaults opened up, and security boxes holding mined raw diamonds were readied for transport. Such days were planned on irregular schedules, and only a handful of people knew when and where and how this was to happen. No other visitors would be allowed that day, and no air traffic was permitted.

There they stood, the missionary pilot, the Italian architect, and the African builder— hands up in the air.

Anton, after a beautiful textbook descent, touched down, rolled out, and turned the plane off the strip onto the grass. They would now find some people and a telephone, he thought. Just then, seemingly out of nowhere, two open jeeps came racing toward the plane and screeched to a halt. Anton and his two passengers alighted from the aircraft, happy for a safe landing, but now staring into the barrels of submachine guns with grim-looking security officers behind them.

"Freeze! Hands up!" was the firm and unfriendly invitation.

There they stood, the missionary pilot, the Italian architect, and the African builder—hands up in the air. What, indeed, was going on? Mine officials accompanied by the security men approached the plane. They had been waiting for a Lear Jet to load four boxes filled with raw diamonds when they saw this strange alien aircraft, our missionary plane, silently approaching the strip. Was this a robbery attempt? Was it to be a diamond heist? It took a lot of talking and detailed explaining before everybody relaxed with relieved laughter following. Then, and only then, were Anton and his passengers received and assisted.

Richard and his two employees were full of praise for their pilot while Anton, nicknamed God's Diamond Smuggler, made one more entry of a happy landing in his logbook.

Voice from the Deep

A speaker? In a latrine? Get the picture?

I scheduled a missionary council meeting at Acornhoek mission in South Africa. Missionaries Ralph McClintock (Brother Mac) and John Wise, stationed at Acornhoek, busily prepared missionary homes for newcomers. Just a few miles away, the Nazarene hospital expected new personnel from overseas. The fellowship was great, spirits were high, and God met with His faithful servants at the mission station.

Acornhoek was not a town, not even a proper village at that time. It had one line for electricity which, at times, had to be supplemented by "homemade" electricity through generators when the main power supply failed to deliver. Only one outpost telephone line serviced the mission station, the hospital, and a number of faraway farmers in the area. Every time a call had to be made, a person would have to crank the old phone, and anyone who was linked to that line could listen in on any conversation.

Of course there were no water closets (WCs) either. Missionaries happily made use of the famous "one-holers," which served the purpose quite efficiently. They just had to be careful, especially at night, to make sure that no unwelcome guests intruded upon them in this snake-invested area.

As Brother Mac and John worked on building two of these latrines for the new homes—which happened to be close to the hall where this council meeting was taking place—they had a grand and rather mischievous idea. Their hope was that it would result in an even more relaxed atmosphere for those who had gathered to discuss God's work in that area.

Brother Mac rigged up a speaker in one of the newly constructed pits and ran a cord with a microphone to the workshop roof close by. John fixed a small sign directing anyone in need of using a facility to the one they had prepared for an appropriate reception.

Mission accomplished. Brother Mac and John retreated to the microphone in the workshop where they sat and waited. Before long one of the famous missionary heroines in South Africa, a lady

Just as she was about to use the convenience, a voice started yelling, "Hey, lady! Hold it! We're still painting down here."

known for her strong opinions, veiled by a charming smile, had to utilize the "resting place." Her name was Irma Koffel. Directed by the freshly painted sign, she decidedly marched to the one that was "mined." Just as she was about to use the convenience, a voice from deep in the pit started yelling, "Hey, lady! Hold it! We're still painting down here."

A mortified missionary came bolting out of that little facility with the speed of a teenager. The commotion, heard by the other council members, caused the victim to hastily retreat to the facility previously used. When she reappeared in the council meeting with her dignity a little tainted, giggling turned to chuckling and soon became hilarity—Irma joining in. After the laughter of all council members had died down, Brother Mac humbly apologized.

How Could I Decline?

On my first exploratory trip to West Africa I found myself in the country of Togo. I landed in Lome and checked myself into a hotel at the outskirts of the city. True to my routine, I bought a map, negotiated a price with a driver, and then went up country for two to three days.

At the conclusion of our journey, we returned to Lome. It was very hot and humid that day, and we still had a long way to go. I asked my driver to find us a place where we could find something to drink to replenish our spent energies. A little later, he stopped at the side of a Togolese kraal—three huts within a square bamboo fencing with one opening. We entered the kraal. Children swarmed all around me, trying to touch my white skin. I looked up and saw my driver conversing in his language with a lady who was busy sweeping the little sandy patch in front of the huts with tree branches. He obviously asked for water. I saw the lady nod and then ask him a question. The driver turned to me.

"The lady is very kind—she will give us some water, but she is also asking if we would like to have something to eat with them."

I pondered the question for a moment. Having had enough of biscuits during the last two or three days, and looking forward to a new experience and something more substantial to eat, I said, "Let's accept the invitation."

A little later we sat in front of one of the huts, the lady making a fire and a man, dressed in not much more than a loincloth, joining the group. Children played in the background. A slow conversation began, my driver interpreting and my French dictionary assisting.

By that time dusk had set in, and the scenario became rather exotic. The trees swallowed up the last rays of the sun. The fire painted pictures of red and orange into the atmosphere. The bamboo fence reflected the light and portrayed spooklike shadows against the wall.

When the man heard that I was from Germany, he smiled and disappeared into one of the huts. When he reappeared, he wore an old and dull-looking cavalry pith helmet from the German Army of the First World War. The headgear was inherited from his grandfather who had been in the German colonial forces of Togoland.

What a picture. His brown glistening chest. The

ragged loincloth. The thin legs with the characteristic flat-footed, broad toes. The pith helmet on his head crowned by a smile that reached from ear to ear. How proud he was to demonstrate and parade this part of his family's treasure, handed down almost 80 years ago. I admit I was impressed.

Surely this is not our dinner tonight, I thought. How mistaken I was.

Just then I glanced over to the other huts and saw a wire that stretched from one pointed roof to the other. Fastened to it by the tails were, what seemed to be, two big rats.

Surely this is not our dinner tonight, I thought. How mistaken I was. A few minutes later the lady clipped the two rats loose, brought them over, and skinned them before my eyes. Leaving the heads on, she put them on the roaster over the open fire. Next to it, a pot of yam and cassava boiled to a stew.

My body's perspiration was now no longer caused just by the temperature of the air, which was still around 95 degrees, but by a premonition that quickly turned into reality.

When all was ready, the children took their places. The driver mentioned to the family that I was a "holy man" and that I would thank God for the food before we ate. He asked me to go ahead and pray.

Was I to thank God for what we were about to receive? Was I to praise Him for feasting us on these two rats? How was I to pray? I thanked Him for a good day and the friendly hospitality and "forgot," conveniently, that I was supposed to pray for the meal.

Then came the worst. Help me! Since I was the special guest, I was rewarded one whole rat while the 14 other people—the driver, father, mother, grandmother, and the children—had to share the second rat.

How I got through this meal I still don't know to this day. While I was chewing—I could not decline this meal without offending these dear people—I thought of the craziest things. Skiing on the slopes of Europe. Holding my wife in my arms. Sitting under the Christmas tree with my children. Facing the general superintendents together with the other regional leaders in Kansas City. Flying my plane. Swimming in the ocean.

Eventually it was finished. All the time I had managed to make conversation, but my mind was somewhere else in this world. Now at last it had come to an end.

The head of the home still proudly wore his German pith helmet while I, close to allowing my stomach to jettison all its intake, wanted to hurry on. Thanking everyone again for their kindness (that was honest) and for a well-prepared meal (that was not quite as honest) I made for the exit and the car now wiser with another African experience!

If anyone asks me today what a rat tastes like, my honest answer is, "Try it. I have absolutely no idea."

Payback with Love

We all agreed. It was payback time.

After serving in Kenya for a few years, missionary David Moyer and his wife, Maryel, returned to Johannesburg, South Africa, to begin new responsibilities in the field office. This gave us the perfect opportunity to "nail" the chief Nazarene prankster of the continent. We knew it had to be done with almost military precision. I called Don Messer, his office team, and the regional office staff for a strategy meeting. All felt that David was long overdue. This was our chance. We devised a plan that called for everyone to cooperate. All were on board.

The Moyers arrived from Kenya in good spirits. We showed them to their new house and threw them a welcome party. As was customary, the missionary family also supplied meals for the first few days.

Soon David and Maryel were back in office, David assisting Don Messer, and Maryel helping with finance and general office work. Two hours into the working day, a police car, with blue lights flashing, screeched to a halt in front of the building. Two police in full gear, including bullet-proof vests, rang the bell. The receptionist in the field office opened the door.

The two police came to David's door, knocked, entered, and asked this trembling missionary to identify himself.

"Does a Mr. David Moyer work in these facilities?"

"Yes. His office is down the corridor."

The two police came to David's door, knocked, entered, and asked this trembling missionary to identify himself. He did. The police produced a summons for arrest, signed and sealed by what looked like a judge. The charge was read. David was accused of having dealt in stolen cars. The Cressida he sold before transferring to Kenya a few years ago had been stolen and used in a robbery attempt.

David pleaded, tried to explain, offered to take them to the car dealer where he purchased the car, pledged to produce the documents of purchase and those of sale—all to no avail.

Don Messer heard the commotion in his office next door and came out. David pleaded with him to put in a word and hopefully convince the police of David's innocence. By that time Maryel had come too. White as a sheet, she also tried to explain. One police officer, handcuffs in hand, apologized again for having to do his duty and approached David. Just then Don Messer suggested that the whole party first see the regional director in his office upstairs. They marched out, David between the two police and the field office staff following.

Mirrored windows line the front of the regional office. As you can imagine, all the employees were glued to these windows as the party marched down the hall, but the staff scurried back to their workplaces before the "parade" arrived. When they entered, the receptionist acted afraid and called me, excitedly speaking about a missionary being arrested and desperately needing help. I promised to come immediately.

First, though, I took a sip of water and hoped that I could keep a straight face. Then I went out to the front. By that time, the whole office staff had closed in, forming a circle around David and Maryel with the two police.

"Richard, please tell these men that you know me, that I am a missionary, and that I would never be involved in a car theft syndicate of which they accuse me."

"Gentlemen, there must be a mistake or error. I have known this man for 15 years. He is a faithful husband, a good father, and an excellent missionary. Please allow him to go back to his office. I will come with you and straighten everything out. There must be an explanation for all of this."

But the police were insistent. Under no circumstances would they allow such a thing. David would have to go to jail, at least until Monday, when the church's attorneys could negotiate bail.

This went on for some time with David calling on just about everybody to put a word in for him. But when I saw Maryel getting tears in her eyes, I thought it had gone far enough.

"David, all of Africa will hear it. This time you were at the short end of things. You have been caught. It is payback time."

David did not hear me. He continued pleading his innocence. But Maryel got it. With great relief she threw her arms around David and gently slapped him on the cheek, saying, "David, it's all a joke." When the truth began to dawn on him, he was so finished, so exhausted, that he had to sit down on the office floor while everybody enjoyed a good laugh.

David learned that the two police were part of the scheme, one of them being the son of my secretary. Even after coffee and tea, it was difficult for everyone to go back to work and be productive again.

Resurrection in a
Mission Hospital

Is it possible to come back from the dead? Consider the following story.

The government of South Africa began negotiating the takeover of all mission-run education and health institutions. It established a policy that gave these institutions to the new homeland (local) governments as incentives for taking responsibility and full control.

The Church of the Nazarene, therefore, entered into negotiations with the newly installed officials at Giyani, the "city in the bush," where the Nazarene mission hospital was located.

Because the church requested compensation, Giyani sent a delegation of health officials and other bureaucrats to inspect the premises, facilities, and equipment at the hospital.

Once again missionary Ralph McClintock (Brother Mac)—a great inventor, innovator, and idea manufacturer on just about any level of church work—endeavored to assist negotiations between the government and the church. That day, the chief medical officer and his staff were ready for the arrival of the inspection team. They even set up the conference room for a tea party after a walk-through of the facilities.

It was then that Brother Mac prepared for his contribution toward a more informal and relaxed gathering by taking the stiffness out of the official reception.

Eight African gentlemen in pin-striped suits and matching ties with stern but friendly faces arrived. Introductions were made and small talk regarding the well-being of each person took its course. Then the tour began. The chief medical officer and the leader of the Giyani delegation led the way as the entourage greeted nurses and patients in the wards. A choir rendered a welcome song. Patients, looking expectantly, received friendly waves and a few nice words.

All the guests suddenly froze. The lid of an oak coffin in front of them slowly lifted.

Thirty-five minutes down the line they had only the mortuary to visit before tea was to be served. The party entered the cool room of the building, each with a solemn expression on his face. A number of bodies were in the drawers awaiting collection by relatives, and a few caskets were on the tables.

All the guests, who had been conversing in subdued tones, suddenly froze. The lid of an oak coffin in front of them slowly lifted on one side. Four knuckles of a white hand appeared, and a voice from within the coffin hoarsely croaked, "Is this heaven . . . or is it the other place?"

The speed with which the Giyani dignitaries exited the building would have rivaled any Olympic sprinter! Dear Brother Mac climbed out of the coffin dusting off his shirt and trousers. Standing mischievously before the chief medical officer he said, "Sorry, sir. I did not think my little performance would have that effect."

As everybody gathered back at the hospital reception, slowly recovering from the "ordeal" and assuming their normal posture again, artificial smiles and jokes made their rounds. It was no wonder that the delegation found itself somewhat pressed for time, thus forfeiting the tea party prepared for them.

The "Secret Weapon" of a Veteran Missionary

When Dr. Jerald Johnson visited Africa for the last time, Harmon Schmelzenbach and I planned a short trip to an island in Lake Victoria to go Nile-perch fishing.

Harmon is an ardent fisherman. His umpteen stories about the size, beauty, and volume of his catches brought many a "flash of envy" to the sanctified ears of other missionaries around campfires during fellowship meetings. Neither Dr. Johnson nor I had ever been Nile-perch fishing. That particular fish, a fine-table meal, is caught by slow-trawling with a lure and can be from one to eight feet in size.

It was a beautiful day. Only a little breeze stirred that morning as we flew out to an island in Lake Victoria. I noticed Harmon carried a little brown paper package under his arm. Jokingly I asked, "Did you bring your lunch along?"

"Richard, this is my special weapon. Just watch tomorrow when we're out on the lake." With that he

An African man with his makeshift boat

opened the package just enough for me to see his shiny lures in metallic blue, turquoise, and green. Most impressive. I had never seen lures like these.

Early the next morning, after a cup of coffee and a light breakfast, we were off with our two-man African crew in an old, beat-up motorboat.

On the way out into the lake, one of the Africans steered the boat while the other asked us if we had ever been fishing before.

"I have been many times," Harmon responded confidently. "But my two greenhorn friends here are in need of instruction and help." We got both. In fact, our African friends handed us the lines and fastened the lures—so different from the ones I had seen the previous day under Harmon's arm. No color, no shine, just plain dented and bent little pieces of aluminum, so they seemed, but the Africans said they would work.

Harmon, all the while, busily prepared his lines, fastening the new lures. I think he prepared about three lines for himself—though I am subject to correction. Far be it from me to exaggerate when describing Harmon. The African fishermen put me on the right side, Dr. Johnson on the left, and Harmon with his three lines in the middle.

Upon reaching what the captain termed the proper fishing ground, we started trawling. I caught the first fish. Not very big, perhaps a two-pounder that we threw back into the water.

Dr. Johnson was next. He got one that was about two-feet long. He, too, was feeling the excitement now. I caught another one, perhaps an eight-pounder. Then Dr. Johnson again. Soon I had a really big one that seemed about five or six feet long. That one was really fighting. Our African friends showed me how to play the fish and slowly bring it in. Eventually it was right next to the boat. Just as we wanted to gaff it, it broke line and got away. I had a new lure fixed and threw it back into the water.

In the meantime, Dr. Johnson had pulled two or

three very nice fish out again. By that time, with our baskets almost full, we looked over to Brother Harmon—he still had to catch his first fish. "I'm watching your lines as well," he said with a smile, "so I don't take much notice of my own." The rather painful smirk on his face spoke louder than his words.

We looked over to Brother Harmon—he still had to catch his first fish.

The day ended with fish of all sizes caught by Dr. Johnson and myself with Harmon still looking for the first one. I shall never forget Harmon's face when we were on land again. With a scale fixed to the branch of a tree, the Africans weighed our catches. The biggest one was a 31-pounder caught by the general superintendent. Harmon just stood there, a sour smile on his face.

Neither Dr. Johnson nor I referred to the misfortune of Harmon, that is, until Sunday back in Nairobi. We were to celebrate our first ordination service in Kenya. The church was packed, the ordinands lined up, and everything was ready.

After some singing and preliminaries, I introduced Dr. Johnson. He entered the pulpit. And then it came. He relayed the story of the day before. Dr. Johnson just couldn't keep quiet about it and gave an almost minute-by-minute report. The congregation roared with laughter.

Suddenly Harmon, sitting next to me on the platform, got up—he could not sit still any longer. He came up to the pulpit, stood next to Dr. Johnson, and began addressing the congregation in true Schmelzenbach fashion.

"Dr. Johnson is right in all he said. But what he did not know or could not understand was the fact that neither he nor Dr. Zanner had ever fished on Lake Victoria. So I made it my responsibility and job to look after their accomplishments rather than my own. That is the reason why my basket remained empty."

Dr. Johnson had to calm the congregation down again after this demonstration of selfless demeanor before he could read the scripture and preach. The collective chuckle went on for quite some time. Nevertheless, Harmon was a sport and took it on the chin.

I have always wondered since then what he did with his "secret weapon."

Scared and Scarred, but Alive!

I never knew I could climb a tree so fast. And a thorn tree at that!

It was a hot, humid Thursday afternoon in Hwange Game Reserve, about 200 miles northwest of Bulawayo, Zimbabwe. I had met with a volunteer from a sister denomination, an expert in deep-drill boreholes and water conservation. I wanted to negotiate a possible project for our church in South Africa, and this engineer from the United Kingdom (UK) had been recommended to me.

On this particular day he and I, along with his family, toured the Hwange game and safari areas, known for its abundance of large animals, especially elephant herds.

After lunch at the game reserve lodge we met on business. I planned to drive back to Bulawayo later to catch my return flight to Johannesburg.

Our talks extended until late afternoon. My new friend thought it might be wiser for me to stay

An elephant herd in Africa

overnight rather than leave that late with only one car and no companion. We were, after all, deep in the bushveld.

"No problem. There is a difference between a tourist and somebody with years of experience in Africa as I have," I responded confidently.

After a hearty farewell, I drove off, savoring the picturesque drive past grazing impala and browsing giraffe on my way to the main road, about 12 miles away from the lodge.

Suddenly the car began to slide, almost floating over the bush track, which became more sandy by the second. I realized that I had taken the wrong turn, being deep in thought about my discussion with the engineer.

I stopped, backed up a little off the track to turn and . . . nothing! Wheels spinning, the engine howling, I tried and tried again. The wheels sank deeper into the sand. I got out of the car and surveyed my situation only to find the car's differential resting solidly on sand. I was stuck!

Observing the immediate surroundings, I checked for unfriendly predators in this lion-infested area. I began digging with my wheel spanner, all to no avail. Then I collected leaves and branches from nearby bushes to make a strip for the tires to find some traction. I tried again. Still no success. What now? I was deep in the bush about three miles from the lodge. Would someone still come by that evening? Would anybody venture out on a sandy trail like this?

I didn't have much time left before nightfall. Should I opt to stay in the car or try to make it on foot to the lodge, about an hour's brisk walk if all went well? I thought of the impala; they could outrun a lion if they had to. I thought of the giraffe I had seen; it could kick a lion and break its jaw should it become necessary. What did I have that I could defend myself with if I needed to?

I took heart, opened my pocketknife, my perennial African companion, and put my wallet with air tickets, money, and passport in my jacket pocket. I then made sure that the car was locked (baboons and monkeys can be rather ingenious when they are hungry) and proceeded back the way I had come.

Was I nervous? No, I was scared! My senses were on red alert, and I moved as quickly as I could. The impala were still grazing, and it seemed to me that some of them lifted their heads, looking at the strange picture of a crazy European with pocket-knife in hand who hurried through the bush.

Suddenly I froze. About 30 yards away and staring straight at me was a rhino female with a calf.

About 300 yards away on my left a small herd of buffalo stood and stared. They had heard me rumbling through the shrub and looked at me with that rigid, almost frozen gaze to which they are accustomed. Wow! Buffalos are dangerous animals, especially when they are wounded. But they were not wounded. They just stood there. And it was not a big herd either. About 15 of them. After all, only the lone excommunicated male is the one that you have to look out for . . . at least that's what the book says. I desperately hoped those species had read the same book. Carefully, I made a big radius around them and strove on.

I was about 35 minutes under way when suddenly I froze. About 30 yards away and staring straight at me was a rhino female with a calf. Out of the corner of my eyes, I surveyed my surroundings and discovered an old African thorn tree close by.

This could provide me with a possible, but very painful, escape route should it become necessary. There they stood, mother and child, two thick-skinned beasts. When the young one moved a little to the side, the mother snorted, still looking at this strange two-legged, ape-like creature armed with a pocketknife.

I knew that rhinos couldn't see very well, but their hearing was excellent. So I just stood still, hoping that the two would move away after a while. I do not know what it was, perhaps my shaking knees banging against each other, perhaps my cramping arms beginning to move, but all of a sudden the mother charged, and so did I. Dropping my pocketknife, I was over there in a shot, climbing that thorn tree as fast as I could with mother now snorting and scratching the sand with her front feet about 10 feet below me. Holding on for dear life and panting like an antelope that had just escaped the jaws of a lion, I hugged the tree trunk, wasting no thought on the 1½-inch-long thorns that caused little trickles of blood to flow down my thighs and my biceps.

After a while, the two unwelcome visitors began trotting off. After all, this two-legged creature was not only apelike, it must have been an ape, having clambered up a thorn tree that fast. I waited another 20 minutes or so and then, conscious of the thorns that had caused deep gashes in my legs and arms, I made my way to the ground.

Collecting my pocketknife and suspiciously looking as if I had a dozen eyes, I continued on my way. I still saw two elephants in the distance, but thankfully no lions, and arrived back at the lodge just as the sun was about to sink into the horizon.

I admit that this was one of the less glamorous experiences I had in my 20 years as regional director for the church in Africa. That evening, having to face my new friend from the UK again, having to reflect on my speech about the difference between a tourist and someone with many years of experience, I was embarrassed to no end. In fact, except for a few people, this is the first time I have shared this story to a wider circle. I still carry the scars. I still tremble when I think of the experience, and I know that I have become wiser and smarter because of that day.

My friend, the true English gentleman he is, never once brought the matter up again. In fact, he has never even joked about it, at least not to me. But I *am* sure he was amused at the picture of the regional director of the Church of the Nazarene in Africa scaling a tree with the speed of a baboon.

Pronunciation Guide

The following information will assist in pronouncing some unfamiliar words in this book. The suggested pronunciations, though not always precise, are close approximations of the way the terms are pronounced.

Introduction

Zanner   ZAN-ner

Chapter 1

Lanseria   Lan-SE-ri-ah

Chapter 2

Abak   A-bak

Calabar   KA-la-bah

Lagos   LAY-gohs

Chapter 3

Ekaidem   E-kei-dem

Udoh   YEW-doh

Chapter 4

Jambo   CHAM-boh

Lilongwe   Li-LONG-we

Chapter 5

Ciskei   SIS-kei

Khosa   KOH-sa

Chapter 6

Anton Hol   AN-tuhn HAHL

Chapter 7

Acornhoek   AY-kern-ook

Chapter 8

Kraal   KRAWL

Lome   LOH-me

Togo   TOH-goh

Chapter 10

Giyani   Gi-AHN-ee

Chapter 11

Schmelzenbach   SHMEHL-zhuhn-bah

Chapter 12

Bulawayo   Boo-lah-WAY-oh

Hwange   WAN-ge